A

Literature Unit

for

A Wrinkle in Time

by Madeleine L'Engle

Written by John and Patty Carratello

Illustrated by Theresa Wright

Teacher Created Materials, Inc.
P.O. Box 1040
Huntington Beach, CA 92647
©*1991 Teacher Created Materials, Inc.*
Made in U.S.A.

ISBN 1-55734-403-5

Table of Contents

Introduction

A good book can touch our lives like a good friend. Within its pages are words and characters that can inspire us to achieve our highest ideals. We can turn to it for companionship, recreation, comfort, and guidance. It also gives us a cherished story to hold in our hearts forever.

In Literature Units, great care has been taken to select books that are sure to become good friends!

Teachers who use this literature unit will find the following features to supplement their own valuable ideas.

- Sample Lesson Plans
- Pre-reading Activities
- A Biographical Sketch and Picture of the Author
- A Book Summary
- Vocabulary Lists and Suggested Vocabulary Activities
- Chapters grouped for study, with each section including:
  - *quizzes*
  - *hands-on projects*
  - *cooperative learning activities*
  - *cross-curriculum connections*
  - *extensions into the reader's own life*
- Post-reading Activities
- Book Report Ideas
- Research Ideas
- A Culmininating Activity
- Three Different Options for Unit Tests
- Bibliography
- Answer Key

We are confident that this unit will be a valuable addition to your planning, and hope that as you use our ideas, your students will increase the circle of "friends" that they can have in books!

Sample Lesson Plan

Each of the lessons suggested below can take from one to several days to complete.

LESSON 1

- Introduce and complete some or all of the pre-reading activities found on page 5.
- Read "About the Author" with your students. (page 6)
- Read the book summary with your students. (page 7)
- Introduce the vocabulary list for SECTION 1. (page 8) Ask students to find all possible definitions for these words.

LESSON 2

- Read Chapters 1 through 3. As you read, place the vocabulary words in the context of the story and discuss their meanings.
- Play a vocabulary game. (page 9)
- Observe the characteristics of five-year-olds. (page 11)
- Find ways to build self-esteem instead of tearing it down. (page 12)
- Discuss the book in terms of science. (page 13)
- Begin "Reading Response Journals." (page 14)
- Administer the SECTION 1 quiz. (page 10)
- Introduce the vocabulary list for SECTION 2. (page 8) Ask students to find all possible definitions.

LESSON 3

- Read Chapters 4 and 5. Place the vocabulary words in context and discuss their meanings.
- Play a vocabulary game. (page 9)
- Demonstrate travel in the fifth dimension. (page 16)
- Make flip books that show metamorphosis. (page 17)
- Discuss the book in terms of math. (page 18)
- Identify and evaluate past and present heroes. (page 19)
- Administer SECTION 2 quiz. (page 15)
- Introduce the vocabulary list for SECTION 3. (page 8) Ask students to find all possible definitions.

LESSON 4

- Read Chapters 6 and 7. Place the vocabulary words in context and discuss their meanings.
- Play a vocabulary game. (page 9)
- Plan a day of "sameness." (page 21)
- Try to bounce balls and jump rope in rhythm. (page 22)
- Discuss the book in terms of social studies. (page 23)
- Discuss the possibilities of what individual students can be. (page 24)
- Administer SECTION 3 quiz. (page 20)
- Introduce the vocabulary list for SECTION 4. (page 8) Ask students to find all possible meanings.

LESSON 5

- Read Chapters 8 and 9. Place the vocabulary words in context and discuss their meanings.
- Play a vocabulary game. (page 9)
- Experiment with the properties of matter. (page 26)
- Stage a debate on issues pertinent to the story. (page 27)
- Discuss the book in terms of science. (page 28)
- Identify and discuss the pressures to conform and the effects of conformity. (page 29)
- Administer SECTION 4 quiz. (page 25)
- Introduce the vocabulary list for SECTION 5. (page 8) Ask students to find all possible meanings.

LESSON 6

- Read Chapters 10 through 12. Place the vocabulary words in context and discuss their meanings.
- Play a vocabulary game. (page 9)
- Conduct a physical inventory of class favorites. (page 31)
- Present story scenes from a different point of view. (page 32)
- Discuss the book in terms of art. (page 33)
- Examine personal choices for dilemmas posed in the story. (page 34)
- Administer SECTION 5 quiz. (page 30)

LESSON 7

- Discuss any questions your students may have about the story. (page 35)
- Assign book report and research projects. (pages 36 and 37)
- Begin work on a culminating activity. (pages 38, 39, 40, and 41)

LESSON 8

- Administer one, two, and/or three unit tests. (pages 42, 43, and 44)
- Discuss the test answers and possibilities.
- Discuss the students' enjoyment of the book.
- Provide a list of related reading for your students. (page 45)

Before the Book

Before you begin reading *A Wrinkle in Time* with your students, do some pre-reading activities to stimulate interest and enhance comprehension. Here are some activities that might work well in your class.

1.   Predict what the story might be about just by hearing the title.

2.   Predict what the story might be about just by looking at the cover illustration.

3.   Discuss other books by Madeleine L'Engle that students may have heard about or read.

4.   Answer these questions:

- •   Are you interested in:
  - – stories about travel through time and space?
  - – stories about children who are extraordinary?
  - – stories that require you to use your imagination and suspend your disbelief?
  - – stories about the power of love?

- •   Would you ever:
  - – invite a very unusual stranger into your house in the middle of the night?
  - – fight to defend members of your family?
  - – travel to a place in time and space that you know nothing about and from which a safe return can not be guaranteed?
  - – stand up to an incredibly powerful adversary when you know your chances of survival are slim?

- •   Have you ever met a person who was truly extraordinary? Describe your experience in detail.

5.   Work in groups or as a class to create your own story of life in another time and space.

About the Author

Madeleine L'Engle Camp was born on November 29, 1918 in New York, New York, to Charles Wadsworth and Madeleine Camp. Her parents exposed her to artistic people and interesting places. She started to write when she was five.

In her childhood, Madeleine enjoyed being alone. Solitude provided her the opportunity to read, dream, and write many stories. As a teenager, Madeleine started to write seriously. Her writing provided entertainment and company.

The family moved to Europe, where Madeleine attended a boarding school. By living in a dormitory she was forced out of her solitary lifestyle. Here she learned to write in the midst of all sorts of distractions. In her later schooling at Ashley Hall in Charleston, South Carolina, she enjoyed herself and was very productive. By her senior year, she was finally a "success" with her peers.

Madeleine went to Smith College and continued her writing. After graduation she lived with several girls in New York. She wrote and looked for acting jobs. It was during this time that her first book, *The Small Rain*, was published. She met Hugh Franklin, an actor whom she married in January of 1946. They moved to Goshen, Connecticut to raise their three children, run a general store, and be a part of the community. Madeleine wrote at night after the children were asleep, but was not able to sell her writing. In spite of the rejection, she knew she would not be happy unless she was writing. In her fortieth year, she began to sell her writing.

In 1963, Madeleine won the Newbery Medal for *A Wrinkle in Time*. Of this book she says:

> *"A writer of fantasy, fairy tale, or myth must inevitably discover that he is not writing out of his own knowledge or experience, but out of something both deeper and wider. I think that fantasy must possess the author and simply use him. I know that this is true of* A Wrinkle in Time. *I can't possibly tell you how I came to write it. It was simply a book I had to write. I had no choice. And it was only after it was written that I realized what some of it meant."*

- "The Expanding Universe"
Horn Book, August, 1963

Some of the other books she has written for children include *Meet the Austins, A Wind in the Door, A Swiftly Tilting Planet, The Time Trilogy, A Ring of Endless Light,* and *Camilla*. Autobiographical accounts include *A Circle of Quiet, The Summer of the Great Grandmother*, and *The Irrational Season*.

Madeleine L'Engle lives and writes in New York and is the volunteer librarian for New York's Cathedral of St. John the Divine. She tours throughout the world speaking. She encourages children to read and establish the habit of regular writing.

Through her books and her speeches, this imaginative writer inspires those who read and hear her words to lead lives that are more open-minded and courageous.

A Wrinkle in Time

By Madeleine L'Engle
(Dell, 1976)

If someone asked you to tesser, could you do it?

It might help you to know that to tesser means to travel through a tesseract—a wrinkle in time. The characters in this story tesser frequently. They move into different times and different worlds in an instant!

When Mr. Murry, a United States physicist, mysteriously disappears, he is deeply missed by his wife and children. After some time, Meg and Charles Wallace, the eldest and youngest of these children, are summoned to the aid of their father by three incredibly eccentric women, who are much more than what they seem.

Led by the strange women and accompanied by a friendly boy named Calvin, the children begin their adventure—an adventure of time and space travel. They move rapidly through a tesseract to several different worlds, finally reaching Camazotz, a world that is clouded by evil, a world in which Mr. Murry is held prisoner. And, in Camazotz, Charles Wallace becomes a captive as well.

What the children do to release Mr. Murry and Charles Wallace from the grasp of evil is suspenseful and thought provoking.

After reading this story, you will know and most likely remember what a tesseract is and what time and space travel might be like.

With what you have learned and experienced, would you be willing to go through a wrinkle in time?

Vocabulary Lists

On this page are vocabulary lists which correspond to each sectional grouping of chapters. Vocabulary activity ideas can be found on page 9 of this book.

SECTION 1
Chapters 1-3

antagonistic	resentment
assimilate	ruffled
avid	scudded
dilapidated	serenity
dubiously	snide
frenzied	subdued
frivoling	subsided
gamboled	supine
inadvertently	sullen
indignantly	tangible
intoned	tesseract
judiciously	tractable
morass	vulnerable
placidly	warily
prodigious	wraithlike

SECTION 2
Chapters 4-5

abruptly	ineffable
axis	inexorable
clarity	mauve
condensed	metamorphose
corporeal	microbe
cosmos	monoliths
dispersed	protoplasm
elliptic	reverberated
enfolded	virtue
ephemeral	void

SECTION 3
Chapters 6-7

aberration	obliquely
arrogance	perspective
bilious	precipitously
bravado	propitious
consistent	remote
diverting	resilience
eon	seethe
furtive	solidify
impressionable	talisman
malignant	unsubstantial
myopic	wheedled
nondescript	writhe

SECTION 4
Chapters 8-9

annihilate	ominous
brusquely	omnipotent
cloven	pedantic
connotations	pinioned
deviate	revelation
dias	sadist
emanate	somber
gait	spindly
gibberish	swivet
grimace	systole
implored	tentatively
insolent	translucent
loftily	transparent
miasma	wrenched
misconception	wryly

SECTION 5
Chapters 10-12

acute	corrosive	formidably	reiterating
appallingly	despondency	imperceptible	reproving
assuaged	disintegration	indignation	temporal
atrophied	emanate	opaque	trepidation
catapulted	fallibility	permeating	vestige

8

Vocabulary Activity Ideas

You can help your students learn and retain the vocabulary in *A Wrinkle in Time* by providing them with interesting vocabulary activities. Here are a few ideas to try.

- ❑ People of all ages like to make and solve puzzles. Ask your students to make their own **Crossword Puzzles** or **Wordsearch Puzzles** using the vocabulary words from the story.

- ❑ Challenge your students to a **Vocabulary Bee!** This is similar to a spelling bee, but in addition to spelling each word correctly, the game participants must correctly define the words as well.

- ❑ Play **Vocabulary Concentration.** The goal of this game is to match vocabulary words with their definitions. Divide the class into groups of 2-5 students. Have students make two sets of cards the same size and color. On one set have them write the vocabulary words. On the second set have them write the definitions. All cards are mixed together and placed face down on a table. A player picks two cards. If the pair matches the words with its definition, the player keeps the cards and takes another turn. If the cards don't match, they are returned to their places face down to the table, and another player takes a turn. Players must concentrate to remember the locations of words and their definitions. The game continues until all matches have been made. This is an ideal activity for free exploration time.

- ❑ Have your students practice their writing skills by creating sentences and paragraphs in which multiple vocabulary words are used correctly. Ask them to share their **Compact Vocabulary** sentences and paragraphs with the class.

- ❑ Ask your students to create paragraphs which use the vocabulary words to present **History Lessons** that relate to the time period or historical events mentioned in the story.

- ❑ Challenge your students to use a specific vocabulary word from the story at least **10 Times In One Day.** They must keep a record of when, how, and why the word was used!

- ❑ As a group activity, have students work together to create an **Illustrated Dictionary** of the vocabulary words.

- ❑ Play **20 Clues** with the entire class. In this game, one student selects a vocabulary word and gives clues about this word, one by one, until someone in the class can guess the word.

- ❑ Play **Vocabulary Charades.** In this game, vocabulary words are acted out!

You probably have many more ideas to add to this list. Try them! See if experiencing vocabulary on a personal level increases your students' vocabulary interest and retention!

Quiz Time!

1. On the back of this paper, write a one paragraph summary of the major events in each chapter of this section. Then complete the rest of the questions on this page.

2. How does Meg feel about herself?

    _____

    _____

3. What kind of a student is Meg in school?

    _____

    _____

4. In one well-written sentence, characterize Charles Wallace.

    _____

    _____

    _____

5. Where is Mr. Murry?

    _____

    _____

    _____

6. Describe the relationship that exists between Meg and Charles Wallace.

    _____

    _____

7. On the back of this paper, describe Mrs. Whatsit, Mrs. Who, and Mrs. Which.

8. In one well-written sentence, characterize Calvin O'Keefe.

    _____

    _____

    _____

9. Define ''sport'' as it is used in *A Wrinkle in Time*.

    _____

    _____

10. Are you more like Meg, Sandy, Dennys, Charles Wallace, Calvin, Mr. Murry, Mrs. Murry, Mr. Jenkins, or the postmistress? Explain who and why on the back of this paper.

I'm Five!

Charles Wallace Murry is not a typical five-year-old child. In fact, there are probably very few, if any, like him in the whole world!

What is a typical five-year-old child like? How does he speak? What types of large and small motor skill abilities are "normal"? How does she interact with others? With what degree of sophistication does this child think?

For this activity, you will observe a small group of five-year-old children. The children you select must be observed in a casual way in an environment which is comfortable for them. Watch these children at least three different times in a variety of situations. Record your observation data for each child on a chart such as this one.

OBSERVATION OF FIVE-YEAR-OLD

Bobby Greenwood *(name)*   Kindergarten Room *(place)*   May 10 *(date)*

BEHAVIOR OBSERVED	EXAMPLE OR COMMENT
Large Motor Skills	**Caught ball easily five times**
Small Motor Skills	**Could print name, backwards "b"**
Language Development	**"Me want ball. Gimme it!"**
Social Skills	**Took ball away from child roughly**
Self-Concept	**Painted a smiling picture of self**
View of Authority	**Obeyed teacher quickly every time**
Conflict management	**Used force rather than words to obtain the ball he wanted**
Ability to Communicate	**Easily understood by peers**
Thinking Skills	**Manipulated Unifix cubes easily to solve a mathematics problem**

After you have finished recording your observations, make a data sheet for Charles Wallace Murry. How do the five-year-olds you have seen compare with Charles Wallace?

One Good Thing

Meg is greatly affected by the things others say and think about her and her family members. She is the victim of "put-downs" by adults in her school, her peers, and even her twin brothers.

"Really, Meg, I don't understand how a child with parents as brilliant as yours are supposed to be can be such a poor student. If you don't manage to do a little better, you'll have to stay back next year."

-Meg's teacher

"Do you enjoy being the most belligerent, uncooperative child in school?"

-the school principal, Mr. Jenkins

"After all, Meg, we aren't grammar-school kids any more. Why do you always act like such a baby?"

-a girl at school

"I wish you wouldn't be such a dope, Meg."

-Meg's brother, Sandy

If it were not for the love, encouragement, and acceptance her mother, father, and youngest brother gave her, she would have nothing on which to build a positive self-concept.

The development of a positive self-concept is critical for the well-being of any person, especially as he or she is growing up. If we don't feel good about ourselves, it is difficult to feel good about anything we say, do, or think.

It is important to help others feel good about themselves whenever we can. For this activity, you and your classmates will do just that!

- Divide into groups of three or four.

- Distribute a paper like the example on the right to every group member.

- Write one "good" thing about every person in your group on your paper. The compliment may relate to a person's eye color, athletic ability, level of kindness, or degree of intelligence. You may write anything, as long as it is complimentary.

- Share what you have written with the members of your group, specifically addressing the complimented member.

- Extend this activity to others, too!

One Good Thing

Name:_____
Good Thing:
_____

Name:_____
Good Thing:
_____

Name:_____
Good Thing:
_____

Science

Mrs. Murry conducted laboratory experiments in her lab at home and, much to the horror of Sandy and Dennys, would often cook the family dinner on the laboratory Bunsen burner. The twins thought that some chemicals might work their way into the food!

The boys would be happy to know that there are experiments you can do using ingredients you find in your kitchen! Here are two for you to try.

REMEMBER THE SOAP!

Soap and water clean away dirt better than just water alone. The reason is that dirt sticks to dishes and hands because of a thin layer of oil or grease. Soap molecules surround the oil or grease molecules and break them apart, allowing them to be washed away more easily because they are separated from each other. Try this experiment to see how.

Materials: Two small jars with screw tops; water; dish soap; cooking oil; measuring tools

Procedure: Put about a half-cup of water and a quarter-cup of oil in each of the jars. Add one-half teaspoon of dish soap to one of the jars. Screw the lids on tightly and shake both the jars. Describe what happens.

Results: Oil and water do not mix in either jar. In the soap jar, the soap keeps the oil from clumping together again, long enough to be washed off.

FIZZ, FOAM, SPUTTER, AND POOF!

New chemicals can form when you mix a few simple ingredients you can find in your kitchen. Try this experiment to see how.

Materials: Wide-mouthed jar; tablespoon of baking soda; teaspoon of vinegar; long match or candle

Procedure: Place the baking soda in the jar. Splash the vinegar over it. With permission, light the match and lower it carefully into the jar.

Results: The vinegar makes the baking soda fizz. The gas (carbon dioxide) released when the vinegar was added to the baking soda puts out the flame. Fire cannot burn with carbon dioxide present.

Do more experiments using household ingredients. Be sure to have your parents' permission and proceed with caution! (See Bibliography on page 45 for ideas.)

Reading Response Journals

One great way to insure that the reading of *A Wrinkle in Time* touches each student in a personal way is to include the use of Reading Response Journals in your plans. In these journals, students can be encouraged to respond to the story in a number of ways. Here are a few ideas.

- Ask students to create a journal for *A Wrinkle in Time*. Initially, just have them assemble lined and un-lined three-holed paper in a brad-fastened report cover with a blank page for the journal's cover. As they read the story, they may draw a design on the cover that helps tell the story for them.

- Tell them that the purpose of the journal is to record their thoughts, ideas, observations, and questions as they read *A Wrinkle in Time*.

- Provide students with, or ask them to suggest, topics from the story that would stimulate writing. Here are a few examples from the chapters in SECTION 1.
  - Meg feels that she does everything wrong and has no redeeming qualities. Describe how you feel about yourself.
  - The Murry family is different from many other families in the town in which they live. How is your family the same as and different from other families you know?
  - Meg feels that much of what she has to learn in school is unimportant. How do you feel about what you have to learn in school?

- After the reading of each chapter, students can write one or more new things they learned in the chapter.

- Ask students to draw their responses to certain events or characters in the story, using the blank pages in their journals.

- Tell students that they may use their journals to record ''diary-type'' responses that they may want to enter.

- Encourage students to bring their journal ideas to life! Ideas generated from their journal writing can be used to create plays, debates, stories, songs, and art displays.

- Allow students time to write in their journals daily.

See the answer key for ideas for the evaluation of your students' Reading Response Journals.

Quiz Time!

1. On the back of this paper, write a one paragraph summary of the major events that happen in each of the chapters in this section. Then complete the rest of the questions on this page.

2. Describe what Meg feels the first time she travels by "wrinkling" through time.

   _____

   _____

   _____

3. What is the black thing that Mrs. Whatsit shows the children on Uriel?

   _____

   _____

4. In what dimension is a tesseract?

   _____

   _____

5. To the best of your ability, explain what a tesseract is. Use the back of this paper for your explanation.

6. Why can't the children breathe as they are about to materialize on a second dimensional planet?

   _____

   _____

   _____

7. Why won't Mrs. Murry and Mrs. O'Keefe miss their children as they travel to other worlds?

   _____

   _____

   _____

8. Can Mrs. Whatsit's age be counted in trillions, billions, millions, thousands, or hundreds of Earth years?

   _____

   _____

9. What does the Happy Medium show the children about Earth that frightens them?

   _____

   _____

10. Who are the fighters from Earth? Do you agree with the children's choices? What fighters would you add to their list? Explain your answers to these questions on the back of this paper.

Show Me How To Tesser!

Meg has difficulty understanding the concept of how they can tesser, or wrinkle, through time. Mrs. Whatsit decides to show her how it can be done, because, as Mrs. Who so appropriately quotes from Cervantes, ''Experience is the mother of knowledge.''

Draw your understanding of the concept of tesser travel on this page. You may use the example that is given in the book or one of your own. Then, physically demonstrate how it can be done using a method similar to the way in which Mrs. Whatsit and Mrs. Who use to show Meg.

Metamorphosis!

The children are awe-struck as they watch Mrs. Whatsit metamorphose into a different being. Here is an interpretation of what they might have seen.

Work in groups of two or three to color and cut out the above pictures. When you have finished, arrange them in numerical order, with number 1 on top. Staple the pictures together along the left side on the staple marks indicated. Flip through the pages of your book and you will see the metamorphosis of Mrs. Whatsit!

Still working in your groups, select a new subject to metamorphose. Make ten or more drawings, larger than the ones on this page, that gradually show one creature becoming another. Combine your pictures into a flip book and share your changing creature with the class!

Math

Charles and Mrs. Whatsit try to explain the concept of the fifth dimension to Meg and Calvin. They begin by discussing the other dimensions first.

- A line is in the first dimension.

- A line is squared in the second dimension.

- In the third dimension, a flat square is squared, making a cube.

- In the fourth dimension, a cube is squared, but as Meg says, it can't be drawn with a pencil the way the first three are drawn.

- A tesseract, in the fifth dimension, is a squaring of the fourth dimension. Charles says that it is possible in this dimension to travel through space ''without having to go the long way around.''

For this activity, you will draw figures in three dimensions. Here are examples of what you will be asked to do.

Draw a line in the first dimension.

Draw a square in the second dimension.

Draw a square in the third dimension.

Draw a rectangle in the third dimension.

Draw a triangle in the third dimension.

Draw a trapezoid in the third dimension.

Practice drawing these figures. After you have mastered them, try to draw other geometrical shapes in the third dimension, such as a circle, a rhomboid, a heart, or, for an exceptional challenge, a star!

Then, discuss with your teacher the concepts of the fourth and fifth dimensions as presented in *A Wrinkle in Time*. Research these concepts for further information. (See Bibliography, page 45.) Maybe you will, as Meg did, cry out,

> ''I see! I got it! For just a moment I got it! I can't possibly explain it now, but there for a second I saw it!''

The Fighters

"All through the universe it's being fought, all through the cosmos, and my, but it's a grand and exciting battle. I know it's hard for you to understand about size, how there's very little difference in the size of the tiniest microbe and the greatest galaxy. You think about that, and maybe it won't seem strange to you that some of our very best fighters have come right from your own planet, and it's a little planet, dears, out on the edge of a little galaxy. You can be proud that you've done so well."

Mrs. Whatsit tells Charles Wallace, Meg, and Calvin that many who have fought the Dark Thing have come from the planet Earth. Here are some of the great "fighters" the children mention:

Jesus	Rembrandt	Buddha	Pasteur
Bach	Leonardo da Vinci	St. Francis	Schweitzer
Einstein	Shakespeare	Euclid	Beethoven
Gandhi	Madame Curie	Michelangelo	Copernicus

How have these people helped to fight the Dark Thing? Working in groups or as a class, research each of the people on this list. Find out what they did in their lifetimes to qualify them to be on a list of those who brought light into darkness.

If you were to choose a group of ten people who have "fought the darkness," would any of the above names be on your list?

Make your own list of fighters. Decide on a group of ten people who have dedicated their lives to enlightening the world in some way. You may use some of the names that were suggested in *A Wrinkle in Time*, if those people have the qualifications you have determined are important. But, in order for your list to be uniquely yours, be sure to include names of your own choosing for at least half of your list.

1. _____   6. _____
2. _____   7. _____
3. _____   8. _____
4. _____   9. _____
5. _____   10. _____

Share your completed list with the class and be ready to support your choices.

Quiz Time!

1. On the back of this paper, write a one paragraph summary of the major events that happen in each of the chapters of this section. Then, complete the rest of the questions on this page.

2. The Happy Medium shows the children a star in a fight with the Dark Thing. What is the outcome of the conflict?

   _____

   _____

3. What did Mrs. Whatsit used to be? Why did she stop being this?

   _____

   _____

4. Why is it good that the Happy Medium showed Meg her mother?

   _____

   _____

5. Name one of the parting gifts given to the children by Mrs. Whatsit or Mrs. Who.

   _____

   _____

6. What do the Earth children discover is unusual about the mothers and children on the outskirts of Camazotz?

   _____

   _____

7. What is CENTRAL Central Intelligence?

   _____

   _____

8. In one well-written sentence, characterize the man with the red eyes.

   _____

   _____

9. Who does the man with the red eyes find most amusing?

   _____

10. On the back of this paper, explain what you might do if you were told that someone else would be controlling your mind for the rest of your life.

Exercise in Sameness

Even though the people of Camazotz have different clothes and different faces, they all look the same. Everyone is the same as everyone else in the same controlled, robotic way.

> *"Six large doors kept swinging open, shut, open, shut, as people went in and out, in and out, looking straight ahead, straight ahead, paying no attention to the children whatsoever, whatsoever."*

Look around you. Are the people in your classroom different than the people of Camazotz? Brainstorm your differences and write your ideas on the board.

What would it be like in your classroom if everyone in it was taught by a machine-like teacher similar to the one who taught second grade spelling on Camazotz? What if asking questions was always discouraged, even punished? What if no one could express an idea that was different than the idea of the teacher, who, in turn, was told what to teach by somebody else?

Try this experiment in sameness.

For one day, one-half day, or one hour, everyone must behave robotically, including the teacher. All students must watch the teacher at all times, postures must be perfect, answers must be given in complete sentences, hands must be raised for every response, lines must be formed for every activity, and no one must talk out of turn. If possible, plan this day in advance so the students and the teacher can dress as uniformly as possible.

How long can you last like this? Does it make you comfortable or uncomfortable to behave like everyone else? Is school fun like this? Do you feel frustrated because you cannot openly express your ideas? Could you or any of your classmates ever be happy on Camazotz?

Together!

Can you imagine walking out to a playground area where everyone is in perfect rhythm with one another? All balls hit the ground at the same time and are caught at the same time. All flying disks are thrown and caught in rhythm with the balls. All children are swinging up when the balls are caught and down when the balls are bounced. All jump ropes hit the ground and rise from it in rhythm with the balls, swings, flying disks, and children's movements. Impossible as it seems, this is what Meg, Calvin, and Charles Wallace see on Camazotz.

"As the skipping rope hit the pavement, so did the ball. As the rope curved over the head of the jumping child, the child with the ball caught the ball. Down came the ropes. Down came the balls. Over and over again. Up. Down. All in rhythm. All identical. Like the houses. Like the paths. Like the flowers."

Here is a challenge for you and your group of three or four people. On the playground today, practice doing all your athletic activities in rhythm with all the members in your group. It will take a lot of coordination, cooperation, and practice.

If you and your group are successful, join with another group to see if you can synchronize all your movements. If your enlarged group is successful, join another group. Do you think it is possible for your whole class to keep in rhythm with one another?

Try it!

Social Studies

Mrs. Whatsit gives each of the children a talisman to help him/her in confrontation with the Dark Thing. Each talisman is based on a quality already present in the child's personality, a quality that needs only to be recognized and strengthened. For Calvin, she strengthens the ability to communicate with others. For Meg, she strengthens faults, the very faults Meg has struggled unsuccessfully to overcome. And for Charles Wallace, she strengthens the resiliency of youth.

For this activity, you will need ten willing class members whose personalities are well-known by the others in the class. The students in the class will pinpoint a characteristic about each of the volunteers that will be helpful to have in a confrontation against an awesome adversary. All class members will record the person's name and characteristic on a chart such as the one below, and include the reasons why each identified quality is important in a confrontation with an enemy.

Name: **Characteristic:** **Reason:**	**Name:** **Characteristic:** **Reason:**
Name: **Characteristic:** **Reason:**	**Name:** **Characteristic:** **Reason:**
Name: **Characteristic:** **Reason:**	**Name:** **Characteristic:** **Reason:**
Name: **Characteristic:** **Reason:**	**Name:** **Characteristic:** **Reason:**
Name: **Characteristic:** **Reason:**	**Name:** **Characteristic:** **Reason:**

Potential

Meg is startled by the realization that it has not been the real Mrs. Whatsit she has seen, but only a small part of who Mrs. Whatsit really is.

> *"The complete, the true Mrs. Whatsit, Meg realized, was beyond human understanding. What she saw was only the game Mrs. Whatsit was playing; it was an amusing and charming game, a game full of both laughter and comfort, but it was only the tiniest facet of all the things Mrs. Whatsit could be."*

Even though Mrs. Whatsit is a purely fictional character, we are like her in many ways. Many of us play "an amusing and charming game," a game in which we "put on a disguise" for the people for whom we are "performing." Sometimes we only give people a tiny glimpse of the people we are or would like to be.

For this activity, you must be completely honest with yourself. Your teacher will not look at your answers unless you would like him or her to do so. Take this opportunity to get to know yourself a little better.

Write and answer these questions in a private journal.

- Do you ever "put on an act" for others? If you do, describe some of your favorite "roles" and why you "perform" each one.

- How do you think others see you?

- Are you happy with the person that other people see you as?

- Would you choose yourself as a friend? Explain your reasons.

- Do you ever wish that people could know things about your personality that only you and a few others know? If so, what do you want others to know about you?

- Do you ever feel that you are not being the person you want to be or know you can be? Explain your feelings.

Quiz Time!

1. On the back of this paper, write a one paragraph summary of the major events that happen in each of the chapters in this section. Then, complete the questions on the rest of this page.

2. What happens to change Charles Wallace?

   _____

   _____

3. What does Charles Wallace now want for Meg?

   _____

   _____

4. List two things that do not exist on Camazotz that exist on Earth.

   _____

   _____

5. Who is the one mind of Camazotz?

   _____

6. What has happened to the boy who couldn't bounce his ball in rhythm?

   _____

   _____

7. What is the difference between the reactions of Charles Wallace and Meg when they see their father?

   _____

   _____

8. What object helps release Mr. Murry from his transparent column?

   _____

9. In one well-written sentence, describe IT.

   _____

   _____

10. On the back of this paper in one paragraph, explain how Meg is almost lost to IT, and how she is saved.

The Properties of Matter

When on Camazotz, Charles Wallace, Meg, and Calvin are able to pass through doors which seem to have no entry. That is because the walls inside CENTRAL Central Intelligence are made up of atoms which can be rearranged by touch.

Atoms make up most of the things we know in our universe. And atoms are the building blocks of matter. Matter is everywhere! You, the food you eat, and the air you breathe are matter.

Matter comes in three forms—solid, liquid, and gas. Each form has different properties, though all matter is made of molecules and all molecules are made of atoms. Matter that is solid has a definite shape and volume (weight) because the molecules are closely packed together. Matter that is liquid has a definite volume, but because its molecules are not as dense (closely packed) as a solid, it takes the shape of its container. Matter that is gas also has no shape and, like a liquid, it takes the shape of its container. But because the molecules are even less dense, they do not hold together when released.

You will experiment with the three forms of matter: solid, liquid, and gas.

Solids

Concept: Matter has properties that can be described.

In small groups, examine a stick of gum. Make a list of the properties of gum. For example, it is flat, it is the shape of a rectangle, it tastes sweet, it bends, it breaks if you bend it too much, etc. Then, chew your gum, and continue to list properties.

Liquids

Concept: Different types of matter have different densities.

Hypothesize how much salt needs to be added to a glass of water before an egg will float. In general, solids are more dense than liquids, and liquids are more dense than gases. Normally, a hen's egg is more dense than water and, if placed in a container of water, will sink to the bottom. However, if you add salt to the water, the water's density will increase. And, if you continue to add salt to the water, at some point the density of the water will be greater than the density of the egg. When that happens, the egg will float.

Gases

Concept: Gas has weight.

Make a balance with two balloons balancing each side. Then, let the air out of one of the balloons. See what happens to the balance. Why do you think it happened?

Continue your experimentation with matter. Some excellent resources can be found in the Bibliography on page 45.

The Debate

In *A Wrinkle in Time*, many issues arise on which people can have a diversity of opinion. Brainstorm as a class to think of some of these areas that might be subject to debate. List your ideas on the board. Then, choose three of these issues in which you are most interested. Write your choices here.

1. _____

2. _____

3. _____

For this activity, you will work in groups to prepare debates on some or all of the issues you have brainstormed as a class or some of the ideas below. Each group will have a different area to debate, and within the group, all opinions on the subject must be represented. Here is an example.

SUBJECT: Disease on our planet causes suffering.

The group that chooses this topic will divide into the number of teams that corresponds to the number of opinions they have on the topic. Each team will represent a point of view within this topic, as outlined below.

TEAM 1: "We believe that everyone with a disease, even the common cold, should be annihilated, as on Camazotz."

TEAM 2: "We believe only the people with serious, life-threatening diseases should be annihilated, as on Camazotz."

TEAM 3: "We believe that every effort should be made to find the cures for all diseases, and the people who suffer from those diseases should be kept alive in case a cure is found."

TEAM 4: "We believe that people who suffer from disease should have the choice to continue or end their lives."

Here are some more ideas from the story you may want to consider for areas to debate.

- There is no deformity on Camazotz.
- There are no differences on Camazotz.
- There is no unhappiness on Camazotz.
- There is no real happiness on Camazotz.
- There are no wars on Camazotz.
- There are no individuals on Camazotz.

Present your prepared debates for your classmates!

Science

IT is a giant brain. Its pulsing engulfs all who feel the rhythm.

The pulse controls the thoughts and movements of those on Camazotz, including adults at work and children at play.

How much do you know about the brain? Does it pulse? Can it control thoughts and movements? Is it a frightening adversary?

Find out more about the human brain. Here are some suggestions for areas to research.

- Identify the major parts of the brain and explain the function of each.

  - hindbrain
  - midbrain
  - forebrain
  - medulla
  - cerebellum
  - reticular formation
  - neural centers

  - pons
  - thalamus
  - hypothalamus
  - pituitary
  - optic nerve
  - cerebral hemispheres
  - olfactory lobe
  - parietal lobe

  - central fissure
  - lateral fissure
  - temporal lobe
  - cerebral cortex
  - limbic system
  - corpus callosum
  - occipital lobe
  - frontal lobe

- Label this side view of the brain.

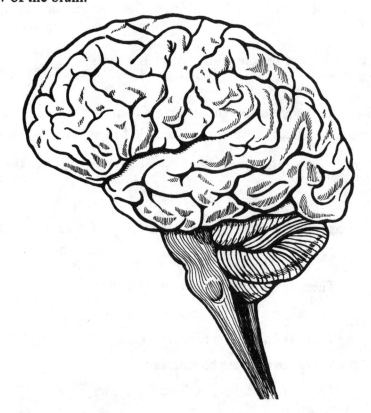

- Label a diagram of a cross section of the brain cut lengthwise. See page 47 for a diagram form to use.

The Pressure To Conform

Meg, Calvin, and Charles Wallace all feel that they need to conform to what is "normal" to be accepted by those around them. Meg struggles with being an "oddball," and agonizes about not fitting in with her schoolmates. Calvin plays basketball to be normal, mostly because he is tall. Charles Wallace decides he should not talk much around others who might perceive him as strange because of the sophistication of his language and thought. He also holds off learning to read because his success at reading would be another indication of his brilliance. They all want to fit in.

But when Charles Wallace is "dissolved" into IT, he tries to convince Meg and Calvin that finally they can have a way to "fit in" and not be different. Their "oddball" days are over if they can just "submit" and lose their individuality in IT. There is an overpowering pressure to conform on Camazotz.

Use your journal to respond to these questions about the pressure to conform.

- What is peer pressure?
- Do you and most of your friends want to be like everyone else?
- How does peer pressure affect you?
- Do you care what others think about you?
- Do you go along with the crowd even though you know what they are doing is wrong?
- Do you do things just because your friends do them, not because you really want to?
- Do you do "popular" things?
- Do you do "unpopular" things?
- Are you more apt to go along with the crowd or follow your own way?
- Would you be more apt to become friends with someone who went along with the crowd, or followed his or her own way?
- Do you say "No!" to your peers if they give you a choice that you know is unwise or wrong?
- Do you act in an uncomfortable way just to be accepted?
- Whose voice has more control over you: yours or your peers'?
- Would you be able to say "No!" to the man with the red eyes?

Quiz Time!

1. On the back of this page, write a one paragraph summary of the main events that happen in each of the chapters in this section. Then, complete the rest of the questions on this page.

2. Who is Meg first to blame for the loss of Charles Wallace?

    _____

3. Why doesn't Mr. Murry grab Charles Wallace as he, Meg, and Calvin tesser away from IT?

    _____

    _____

4. In one well-written sentence, describe the inhabitants of Ixchel.

    _____

    _____

5. Who is Aunt Beast?

    _____

    _____

6. Why does Meg have to be the one to go back to Camazotz and rescue Charles Wallace from IT?

    _____

    _____

7. What gifts do Mrs. Whatsit, Mrs. Who, and Mrs. Which give Meg as she is about to return to Camazotz?

    _____

    _____

    _____

8. Is Charles Wallace himself when Meg returns to Camazotz?

    _____

9. How does Meg pull Charles Wallace away from IT?

    _____

    _____

10. On the back of this paper, predict how things might have been different in the Murry family if Meg had not rescued Charles Wallace.

Inventory

On the planet of Ixchel, Meg, Calvin, and Mr. Murry are introduced to the "beasts" who live there. These creatures provide them with many sensory pleasures. Aunt Beast's body is "covered with the softest, most delicate fur imaginable," the fragrance of the air on the planet and Aunt Beast's fur has the most "beautiful odor," the songs sung by Aunt Beast are "even more glorious than the music of the singing creatures on Uriel," and the food is without compare, or as Calvin puts it, "You've never tasted such food in your life!"

Working as a class, develop sensory-inventory stations. At each station, the students in the class will experience a range of sensory stimulation and decide on what object at the station provides them with the "most pleasurable" experience. Here is an example of what can be included in these stations. Provide the students with graphs to chart their choices for the best sight, smell, sound, taste, or touch at each station.

STATION 1—SIGHT

Contents of station:
- a vase of spring flowers
- a painting of a beautiful scene
- a picture of an alert deer
- an unusually pretty shell
- a peacock's feather

STATION 2—SMELL

Contents of station:
- a loaf of fresh bread
- lilacs
- a bottle of cologne
- chocolate syrup
- a pine branch

STATION 3—SOUND

Contents of station:
- recording of a cricket
- recording of the ocean
- recording of bird songs
- recording of a guitar
- recording of children's laughter

STATION 4—TASTE

Contents of station:
- grapes
- chocolate chips
- peppermint candy
- strawberries
- potato chips

STATION 5 - TOUCH

Contents of station:
- a feather
- animal fur
- velvet
- sand
- a smooth stone

Sample Graph
Best _____

Item					
6					
5					
4					
3					
2					
1					

Point of View

Mr. Murry, Charles Wallace, Meg, and Calvin left their time and space, tessering to a world controlled by an evil, overpowering force. We have all read the outcome of this story.

But suppose the story were to be told in a different way than Madeleine L'Engle chose to tell it. Suppose it was not from Meg's vantage point that the story was created. Would the outcome be the same?

Cut these narrator-choice cards apart and place them in a pile. Divide the class into groups of three or four. Each group will select one representative to choose a card from the pile. The different groups will then work together to recreate and perform a scene of their choice from the story from the point of view represented by the card they have drawn.

STORYTELLER: Mrs. Whatsit	**STORYTELLER:** Mrs. Who	**STORYTELLER:** Mrs. Which
STORYTELLER: Charles Wallace	**STORYTELLER:** Mr. Murry	**STORYTELLER:** Calvin
STORYTELLER: IT	**STORYTELLER:** Fortinbras	**STORYTELLER:** Aunt Beast

Art

Locate all the descriptive references to the inhabitants of Ixchel that you can find in the story. Use the information you find to draw a picture of one of the "beasts" who lives on the dull gray planet.

If You Were There . . .

Suppose you were in the place of one of the characters from *A Wrinkle in Time*. What would you do in each of the following situations? You may share your responses with the class or write them in your journal.

- You have a five-year-old brother who can "read your mind" with unbelievable accuracy.
- Your husband has been gone a very long time and you have not had any word from him for a year.
- The postmistress has been spreading rumors about your family.
- Mrs. Whatsit has just knocked at your door in the middle of the night.
- You are listening angrily to the principal of the school explain just how uncooperative and belligerent you are.
- You are the principal of a high school, tired of complaints about a very uncooperative and belligerent girl.
- You are in eleventh grade. A five-year-old begins an intellectual conversation with you, through which you find out that he is intellectually equal, and perhaps superior, to you.
- You are a five-year-old child who has just been called a moron.
- You are asked to go somewhere you don't know with people you have just met.
- Three unbelievably strange women want you to go on a dangerous mission with them.
- You experience travel through time and space.
- You are a child on Camazotz who does not want to bounce a ball in rhythm with everyone else.
- You are the mother of the child on Camazotz who does not want to bounce his ball in rhythm with all the other children. You know the consequences of deviant behavior.
- You are a second grade spelling teacher who always has to teach spelling in a robotic way.
- You are Charles Wallace, beginning to feel the presense of a very powerful, mind-controlling force.
- You are the man with the red eyes. Charles Wallace has just kicked you.
- You are IT, eager to control some new minds from Earth.
- You meet IT for the first time.
- IT tries to take over your mind.
- Coming toward you are three gray "beasts," with four arms, no eyes, and multi-fingered tentacles.
- You must decide whether or not to face IT again to save the life of your brother. You may not succeed.
- Knowing what it is like to tesser, you have been asked to tesser again.
- Make up your own "If You Were There . . ." situations to answer.

Any Questions?

When you finished reading *A Wrinkle in Time*, did you have some questions that were left unanswered? Write them here._____

_____

_____

_____

Then, work in groups or by yourself to prepare possible answers for the questions you have asked above or some of those written below. When you have finished, share your ideas with the class.

- Where do Mrs. Whatsit, Mrs. Who, and Mrs. Which go and what do they do after the story?
- Do the Murrys and Calvin ever see Mrs. Whatsit, Mrs. Who, and Mrs. Which again?
- Now that Mr. Murry is home, what does the postmistress have to say about his return?
- Does the government expect Mr. Murry to tesser again? Does he want to do it for them?
- Do Meg and Charles Wallace explain their adventures to Sandy and Dennys? If so, do the twins understand and believe them?
- Do Meg and Calvin date?
- Is Meg a better student when she returns to school? Is she belligerent and uncooperative?
- Do Mr. Jenkins and Meg's teachers ever recognize and appreciate Meg's abilities?
- Does Calvin continue to play basketball? Do Meg and her brothers enjoy watching him?
- Does Charles Wallace make any friends his own age?
- How do dead stars become Mrs. Whatsits?
- Does the ball-dropping boy on Camazotz remember the strangers from Earth at all? Does he bounce in rhythm now?
- Just who is the man with the red eyes?
- How does IT feel about Meg and Charles Wallace?
- Does anything change on Camazotz because of Meg's interference?
- Do Meg, Charles Wallace, and Calvin tesser again?
- Does Mrs. Murry join them? Do Sandy and Dennys?
- What happened to Hank, the first of Mr. Murry's group to tesser?
- Can a person be so in tune with another as to anticipate his or her needs and actions?
- Are there such things as tesseracts?
- Do you believe this story could happen sometime, if not now in the future?

Book Report Ideas

There are numerous ways to report on a book once you have read it. After you have finished reading *A Wrinkle in Time*, choose one method of reporting on the book that interests you. It may be a way that your teacher suggests, an idea of your own, or one of the ways that is mentioned below.

• **See What I Read?**

This report is a visual one. A model of a scene from the story can be created, or a likeness of one or more of the characters from the story can be drawn or sculpted.

• **Time Capsule**

This report provides people living at a future time with the reasons *A Wrinkle in Time* is such an outstanding book, and gives these future people reasons why it should be read. Make a time capsule-type of design, and neatly print or write your reasons inside the capsule. You may wish to ''bury'' your capsule after you have shared it with your classmates. Perhaps one day someone will find it and read *A Wrinkle in Time* because of what you wrote!

• **Come To Life!**

This report is one that lends itself to a group project. A size-appropriate group prepares a scene from the story for dramatization, acts it out, and relates the significance of the scene to the entire book. Costumes and props will add to the dramatization!

• **Into the Future**

This report predicts what might happen if *A Wrinkle in Time* were to continue. It may take the form of a story in narrative or dramatic form, or a visual display.

• **A Letter to the Author**

In this report, you can write a letter to Madeleine L'Engle. Tell her what you liked about *A Wrinkle in Time*, and ask her any questions you may have about the writing of the book. You might want to give her some suggestions for a sequel! After your teacher has read it, and you have made your writing the best it can be, send it to her in care of the publishing company.

• **Guess Who or What!**

This report is similar to ''Twenty Questions.'' The reporter gives a series of clues about a character from the story in a vague to precise, general to specific order. After all clues have been given, the identity of the mystery character must be deduced. After the character has been guessed, the same reporter presents another ''Twenty Clues'' about an event in the story.

• **A Character Comes To Life!**

Suppose one of the characters in *A Wrinkle in Time* came to life and walked into your home or classroom? This report gives a view of what this character sees, hears, and feels as he or she experiences the world in which you live.

• **Sales Talk**

This report serves as an advertisement to ''sell'' *A Wrinkle in Time* to one or more specific groups. You decide on the group to target and the sales pitch you will use. Include some kind of graphics in your presentation.

• **Coming Attraction!**

A Wrinkle in Time is about to be made into a movie and you have been chosen to design the promotional poster. Include the title and author of the book, a listing of the main characters and the contemporary actors who will play them, a drawing of a scene from the book, and a paragraph synopsis of the story.

• **Literary Interview**

This report is done in pairs. One student will pretend to be a character in the story, steeped completely in the persona of his or her character. The other student will play the role of a television or radio interviewer, trying to provide the audience with insights into the character's personality and life. It is the responsibility of the partners to create meaningful questions and appropriate responses.

Research Ideas

Describe three things you read in *A Wrinkle in Time* about which you would like to learn more.

1. _____

2. _____

3. _____

As you were reading *A Wrinkle in Time,* you encountered scientific information, space and time travel concepts, diverse and very unusual people, and many ideas that are fantastic but not completely improbable. To increase your understanding of the characters and events in the story as well as recognize more fully Madeleine L'Engle's craft as a writer, research to find out more about these people, places, and things!

Work in groups to research one or more of the areas you named above, or the areas that are mentioned below. Share your findings with the rest of the class in any appropriate form of oral presentation.

- Major fields in biology, such as:
    - Anatomy
    - Bacteriology
    - Biochemistry
    - Botany
    - Ecology
    - Embryology
    - Evolutionary Biology
    - Genetics
    - Immunology
    - Medicine
    - Microbiology
    - Molecular Biology
    - Neurobiology
    - Pathology
    - Physiology
    - Systematics
    (There are many other fields in Biology. These are just a few that may have been of interest to Mr. and Mrs. Murry.)

- Fields of study in Physics:
    - mechanics
    - heat
    - light
    - electricity and magntism
    - sound
    - structure of matter
- Astronomy
    - space travel
    - tesseracts
    - galaxies, such as the Milky Way
    - stars, such as Orion and Malak
    - solar systems
    - planets
    - the speed of light
- Mathematics
- Dimensions
- The human brain (See page 28.)

- historical figures mentioned in the book (See page 19)

Tesseract Adventure!

You have been chosen to cross into the fifth dimension, to travel by tesseract to times and worlds unknown!

For this culminating activity, you will share your tesseract adventure with the class. Here are some projects for you to complete.

- Create a cover sheet for your tesseract adventure presentation. You may use the cover design on page 39.

- Briefly describe the moment you realized that you had been chosen to tesser.

- List the qualities about you that made you the candidate to tesser to an unknown place and time.

- Draw a picture of your guide. At the bottom of the drawing, give a written description of any special characteristics this guide possesses.

- Explain the purpose of your adventure.

- Create the dialogue that occurs between you and your guide as your adventure is planned.

- Describe your thoughts and feelings as you are about to begin your trip into the unknown.

- Describe your journey through the tesseract in detail.

- Write about or illustrate your landing.

- Draw a picture of the setting in which you landed.

- Complete a Personality Profile Sheet for one of the inhabitants of this world. (See page 40.)

- Write your first dialogue with a character from this time and place.

- Explain, and give examples of, the method of communication that is most successful for your use in this world.

- Chart the similarities and differences between your world and this world.

- Explain the success or failure of your mission.

- Explain the reasons you should stay.

- Explain the reasons you should go.

- Describe your re-entry into your time period.

- Construct a collage of experiences you had while tessering that will intrigue and interest your audience. Make them want to find out what happened to you! A sample collage page can be found on page 41.

- Describe the reactions of those to whom you told your story.

- Decide if you would be willing to tesser again. Support your decision clearly.

The
Log of My
First

TESSERACT

ADVENTURE!

by

_____

(Time and Space Traveler)

My Journey to

_____

Took place between the Dates of

_____

Personality Profile Sheet

Planet: _____Time: _____

Inhabitant's Name:_____

Age: _____ Height: _____Weight: _____

Male or Female: _____

Physical Description: _____

_____

_____

Sample of Language: _____

_____

Method of Movement: _____

_____

Food Choices: _____

_____

Recreational Choices: _____

_____

Daily Habits: _____

_____

_____

Degree of Friendliness: _____

_____

Special Notes: _____

_____

_____

Collage of Experiences

On this page, make a collage of experiences that might have happened to a person who has traveled to another world or another time. Be imaginative and have fun!

Unit Test

Matching: Match the quotes with the people who said them.

The Happy Medium	Mr. Murry	Mr. Jenkins	Calvin
Charles Wallace	Mrs. Which	Mrs. Whatsit	Mrs. Who
Aunt Beast	Meg	Mrs. Murry	IT

1. _____ ''Lead on, moron. I've never even seen your house, and I have the funniest feeling that for the first time in my life I'm going home!''

2. _____ ''Alll rrightt, girrllss. Thiss iss nno ttime forr bbickkerring.''

3. _____ ''I know our world isn't perfect, Charles, but it's better than this. This isn't the only alternative! It can't be!''

4. _____ ''I didn't mean to tell you. I didn't mean ever to let you know. But, oh, my dears, I did so love being a star!''

5. _____ ''I have to find out what he really is. You know that. I'm going to try to hold back. I'm going to try to keep part of myself out. You mustn't stop me this time, Meg.''

True or False: Write true or false next to each statement below. On the back of this test paper, explain why each false answer is false.

1. _____ Meg, Sandy, Dennys, and Charles Wallace are all exceptional children.

2. _____ Mr. Murry was not the first from his group to travel by tessaract.

3. _____ The Earth children met the Happy Medium on Uriel.

4. _____ The inhabitants of Ixchel have no sense of sight.

5. _____ Meg is returning to Earth stronger than when she left it.

Short Answer: Provide a short answer for each of these questions.

1. How did Mrs. Murry know something had happened to her husband?_____

2. Who is Fortinbras? _____

3. Which of the three ''ladies'' spoke by using quotations? _____

4. Who controls the minds on Camazotz? _____

5. Why does IT lose Charles Wallace? _____

Essay: Write these essays on the back of this paper.

1. Describe the relationship that exists between Meg and Charles Wallace.

2. Decide if Meg changes her self-concept because of what happened to her in the story. Support your position.

Response

Explain the meaning of each of these quotations from *A Wrinkle in Time*.

Chapter 1:   *"I hate being an oddball,"* Meg said.

Chapter 1:   *"I shall just sit down for a moment and pop on my boots and then I'll be on my way. Speaking of ways, pet, by the way, there is such a thing as a tesseract."*

Chapter 2:   *"I don't understand it any more than you do, but one thing I've learned is that you don't have to understand things for them to be."*

Chapter 3:   *With a sudden enthusiastic gesture Calvin flung his arms out wide, as though he were embracing Meg and her mother, the whole house. "How did all this happen? Isn't it wonderful? I feel as though I were just being born! I'm not alone any more! Do you realize what that means to me?"*

Chapter 3:   *"But you see, Meg, just because we don't understand doesn't mean that the explanation doesn't exist."*

Chapter 3:   *"Charles Wallace is what he is. Different. New."*

Chapter 4:   *"Oh, we don't travel at the speed of anything,"* Mrs. Whatsit explained earnestly. *"We tesser. Or you might say, we wrinkle."*

Chapter 4:   *"That dark thing we saw, is that what my father is fighting?"*

Chapter 5:   *"We took a time wrinkle as well as a space wrinkle."*

Chapter 5:   *"Therre willl nno llonggerr bee sso manyy pplleasanntt thinggss too llookk att iff rressponssible ppeoplle ddo nnott ddoo ssomethingg abboutt thee unnppleasanntt oness."*

Chapter 5:   *"And we're not alone, you know, children,"* came Mrs. Whatsit, the comforter. *"All through the universe it's being fought, all through the cosmos, and my, but it's a grand and exciting battle."*

Chapter 6:   *"I didn't mean to tell you,"* Mrs. Whatsit faltered. *"I didn't mean ever to let you know. But, oh, my dears, I did so love being a star!"*

Chapter 7:   *"You see, what you will soon realize is that there is no need to fight me. Not only is there no need, but you will not have the slightest desire to do so. For why should you wish to fight someone who is here only to save you pain and trouble? For you, as well as for the rest of all the happy, useful people on this planet, I, in my own strength, am willing to assume all the pain, all the responsibiltiy, all the burdens of thought and decision."*

Chapter 8:   *"Oh, Meg, if you'd just relax you'd realize that all our troubles are over. You don't understand what a wonderful place we've come to. You see, on this planet everything is in perfect order because everybody has learned to relax, to give in, to submit."*

Chapter 8:   *"On Camazotz we are all happy because we are all alike. Differences create problems."*

Chapter 8:   *"Maybe if you aren't unhappy sometimes you don't know how to be happy."*

Chapter 12:   *"If we knew ahead of time what was going to happen we'd be—we'd be like the people on Camazotz, with no lives of our own, with everything all planned and done for us."*

Chapter 12:   *"You mean you're comparing our lives to a sonnet? A strict form but freedom within it?"*

              "Yes," Mrs. Whatsit said. *"You're given the form, but you have to write the sonnet yourself. What you say is completely up to you."*

Chapter 12:   *She knew! Love. That was what she had that IT did not have.*

Teacher Note: Choose an appropriate number of quotes for your students.

Conversations

Work in size-appropriate groups to write and perform the conversations that might have occured in each of the following situations.

- Meg, her teacher, Mr. Jenkins, and Mrs. Murry talk about Meg's behavior in school. (4 people)
- The postmistress begins to spread more rumors about the mysterious disappearance of Mr. Murry. Meg, Mrs. Murry, Charles Wallace, and Calvin overhear her. (5 people)
- Sandy and Dennys meet Mrs. Whatsit before Charles Wallace does. (3 people)
- Charles Wallace and Calvin talk about what it is like to be a sport. Meg listens and responds. (3 people)
- Meg tells Calvin why she has difficulty in school. (2 people)
- Mrs. Whatsit, Mrs. Who, Mrs. Which, and Charles Wallace talk about the advisability of taking Calvin and Meg on the trip. (4 people)
- Charles Wallace, Meg, and Calvin discuss why and if they should travel through time and space with the "ladies." (3 people)
- Charles Wallace, Meg, and Calvin discuss tesseracts and the various theories involved. (3 people)
- In the paper-flat way they have of talking, the inhabitants of the planet in the second dimension talk about the visitors from Earth they almost had. (any number of people)
- Mrs. Whatsit explains how she died as a star in her battle with the Dark Thing. The children and her time-traveling friends listen and respond to her story. (4 or more people)
- The ball-playing, rope-jumping, robotic children of Camazotz have a conversation about the things they do for fun. (any number of people)
- A typical spelling lesson is conducted in a second grade classroom on Camazotz. (any number of people)
- The boy who could not bounce in rhythm, his mother, and a Central Intelligence agent discuss the boy's deviant behavior. (3 people)
- Charles Wallace explains to Meg and Calvin how it feels to have his mind taken over. They respond. (3 people)
- Mr. Murry, Meg, and Calvin try to explain to Charles Wallace that IT is the enemy. Charles Wallace responds. (4 people)
- IT takes over the minds of Meg, Calvin, and Mr. Murry. Charles Wallace is there to congratulate their wise decision. (5 people)
- Aunt Beast tells her friends on Ixchel about the "funny little tadpole" named Meg. (3 or more)
- IT stages a very special welcome for Meg's return to Camazotz. (2 or more people)
- Mrs. Whatsit, Mrs. Who, and Mrs. Which, in their own special way of speaking, discuss Meg's victory. (3 people)
- Meg and Calvin start to see each other socially. A fellow basketball player and a girl who thinks Meg is childish voice their opinions to the new couple. (4 people)
- Charles Wallace registers for kindergarten. The principal, the kindergarten teacher, and Mr. and Mrs. Murry are there as well. (5 people)
- The government sends an agent to Mr. Murry to recruit him for more tesser travel. Members of the family and Calvin are there to voice their opinions on the matter. (4 to 8 people)
- Mrs. Whatsit, Mrs. Who, and Mrs. Which tell where they are now going. (3 people)
- Characters from the story talk about how they view Meg. They may or may not interact with each other. Include Charles Wallace, Calvin, Mr. Murry, Mrs. Murry, Mr. Jenkins, IT, Mrs. Whatsit, and Aunt Beast. (8 people)

Write and perform one of your own conversation ideas for the characters from *A Wrinkle in Time.*

Bibliography of Related Reading

Abbott, Edwin. *Flatlands.* (Dover, 1952)

Apfel, Necia H. *It's All Relative: Einstein's Theory of Relativity.* (Lothrop, Lee & Shepard, 1981)

Babbitt, Natalie. *The Search for Delicious.* (Farrar, Straus and Giroux, 1988)

Baldwin, Dorothy and Claire Lister. *Your Brain and Nervous System.* (Bookwright, 1984)

Bradbury, Ray. *The Martian Chronicles.* (Bantam, 1979)

Challand, Helen J., Ph. D. *Activities in the Physical Sciences.* (Regensteiner, 1984)

Dank, Milton. *Albert Einstein.* (Franklin Watts, 1983)

De Saint-Exupery, Antoine. *The Little Prince.* (Scholastic, 1975)

Gardner, Robert. *Kitchen Chemistry.* (Julian Messner, 1988)

Gardner, Robert. *Projects in Space Science.* (Julian Messner, 1988)

Herbert, Don. *Mr. Wizard's Experiments for Young Scientists.* (Doubleday, 1959)

Hogben, Lancelot. *The Wonderful World of Mathematics.* (Doubleday, 1968)

Kalb, Jonah and David Viscott, M.D. *What Every Kid Should Know.* (Houghton Mifflin, 1976)

Kondo, Herbert. *Adventures in Space and Time: The Story of Relativity.* (Holiday House, 1966)

L'Engle, Madeleine.

> The Time Trilogy:
>
>> *A Wrinkle in Time.* (Dell, 1976)
>> *A Wind in the Door.* (Farrar, 1973)
>> *A Swiftly Tilting Planet.* (Farrar, 1978)
>
> This is a partial listing of her other books for children:
>
>> *And Both Were Young.* (Lothrop, 1949)
>> *Meet the Austins.* (Vanguard, 1960)
>> *The Moon by Night.* (Farrar, Straus and Giroux, 1963)
>> *The Twenty-Four Days Before Christmas.* (Farrar, 1964)
>> *The Arm of the Starfish.* (Farrar, 1965)
>> *The Young Unicorns.* (Farrar, 1968)
>> *Prelude.* (Farrar, 1968)
>> *Dance in the Desert.* (Farrar, 1969)
>> *Intergalactic P.S.3.* (Children's Book Council, 1970)
>> *Dragons in the Waters.* (Farrar, 1976)
>> *A Ring of Endless Light.* (Farrar, 1980)
>> *Camilla.* (Delacorte, 1981)
>
> These are her autobiographical works:
>
>> *A Circle of Quiet.* (Farrar, 1972)
>> *The Summer of the Great Grandmother.* (Farrar, 1974)
>> *The Irrational Season.* (Seabury, 1977)

Lewis, C.S. *The Lion, the Witch and the Wardrobe* and others in the The Cronicles of Narnia series. (Collier, 1970)

McGough, Elizabeth. *Who Are You?* (William Morrow, 1976)

McGrath, Susan. *Fun With Physics.* (National Geographic Society, 1986)

McKinley, Robin. *The Hero and the Crown.* (Ace, 1987)

Sabin, Francene. *Microbes and Bacteria.* (Troll, 1985)

Simon, Seymour. *Chemistry in the Kitchen.* (Viking, 1971)

Simon, Seymour. *How To Be A Space Scientist In Your Own Home.* (J.B. Lippincott, 1982)

Winthrop, Elizabeth. *The Castle in the Attic.* (Bantam, 1985)

Zim, Herbert S. *Your Brain and How It Works.* (William Morrow, 1972)

Answer Key

Page 10

1. Accept appropriate responses.

2. Meg has very low self-esteem. She thinks she is ugly and quite an oddball.

3. Meg causes trouble in school. She does not see the importance of some of what she is asked to do in school. She is also defensive and belligerent.

4. Accept appropriate responses.

5. Mr. Murry, on a top secret "mission" for the United States government, has disappeared.

6. Meg and Charles Wallace are close and Charles Wallace can "read" Meg's needs. He is tuned into her. Meg loves her brother deeply and is very protective of him.

7. Accept reasonable answers. There is a description of Mrs. Whatsit in Chapter 1, Mrs. Who in Chapter 2, and an initial description of Mrs. Which in Chapter 3.

8. Accept reasonable answers.

9. A sport is a person for whom a specific characteristic that is not present in the parents is present in him or her.

Page 14

Explain to the students that their Reading Response Journals can be evaluated in a number of ways. Here are a few ideas.

• Personal reflections will be read by the teacher, but no corrections or letter grades will be assigned. Credit is given for effort, and all students who sincerely try will be awarded credit. If a "grade" is desired for this type of entry, you could grade according to the number of journal entries for the number of journal assignments. For example, if five journal assignments were made and the student conscientiously completes all five, then he or she should receive an "A."

• Non-judgmental teacher responses should be made as you read the journals to let the students know that you are reading and enjoying their journals. Here are some types of responses that will please your journal writers and encourage them to write more. "You have really found what's important in the story!"; "WOW! This is interesting stuff!"; "You write so clearly, I almost feel as if I am there!"; "You seem to be able to learn from this book and apply what you learn to your life!"; "If you feel comfortable doing so, I'd like you to share your idea with the class. They will enjoy what you've written!"

• If you would like to grade something for form and content, ask the students to select one of their entries and "polish it" according to the writing process.

Page 15

1. Accept appropriate responses.

2. There is nothing to feel.

3. The black thing is the "power of evil."

4. A tesseract is in the fifth dimension.

5. Accept all reasonable attempts.

6. In a second dimensional world, everything is flat like paper, including the children's lungs.

7. The children take a time and space wrinkle, and will only be gone from the Earth about five minutes.

8. Mrs. Whatsit's age can be measured in billions of years.

9. The Happy Medium shows the children that the Earth is shrouded by the Dark Thing.

Page 20

1. Accept appropriate responses.

2. The star wins over the darkness, but loses its own life in the process.

3. Mrs. Whatsit was a star who lost her star life fighting the Dark Thing.

4. Because Meg saw her mother sad and distraught, she got angry at whatever it was that caused the loss of her father. She realized that she can't be scared when she's angry.

5. Accept any correct choice.

6. The mothers and children who live in the outskirts all act and look the same, except for the boy who lost his "bounce."

7. CENTRAL Central Intelligence is the main headquarters for the planet.

8. Accept appropriate responses.

9. Meg is most amusing.

Page 25

1. Accept appropriate responses.

2. The power behind the man with the red eyes has "taken him in."

3. Charles Wallace wants his sister to join him by being taken in by the man with the red eyes.

4. Accept appropriate responses, such as no illness, disease, or deformity, no wars or unhappiness, and no differences.

Answer Key *(cont.)*

Page 25 *(cont.)*

5. IT is the one mind of Camazotz.

6. The boy is being punished for deviating from the rest of the children.

7. Accept appropriate responses.

8. Mrs. Who's glasses help Mr. Murry.

9. Accept appropriate responses.

10. Accept appropriate responses.

Page 28

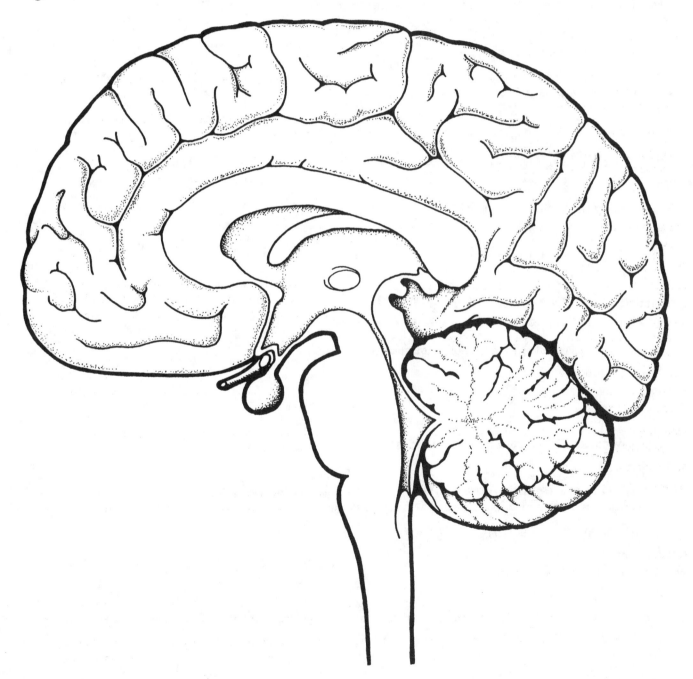

Answer Key *(cont.)*

Page 30

1. Accept appropriate responses.

2. Meg thinks Mr. Murry is to blame for the loss of Charles Wallace.

3. IT has too much control over Charles Wallace and if he had been brought back, his brain may have suffered irreparable damage.

4. Accept appropriate responses.

5. Aunt Beast is the inhabitant of Ixchel who nourishes and guides Meg back to health.

6. Meg is the one who is closest to Charles Wallace and he understands and trusts her.

7. Mrs. Whatsit gives Meg her love, Mrs. Who gives Meg a quote to build her self-esteem, and Mrs. Which gives her the knowledge that Meg has something IT does not that can be used as a weapon against IT.

8. IT is even in more control of Charles Wallace then when she left.

9. With her love she pulls him away.

Pages 38 to 41

Create a bulletin board display of these culminating activities.

Page 42

Matching

1) Calvin 2) Mrs. Which 3) Meg 4) Mrs. Whatsit 5) Charles Wallace

True or False

1. False; Sandy and Dennys are "normal."

2. True

3. False; They met her on another planet.

4. True

5. True

Short Answer

1. She had received no letters from him for over a year.

2. The Murry's dog

3. Mrs. Who

4. IT

5. The power of love is too strong for IT. (or a similar response)

Essay

1. Accept appropriate responses. Answers should reflect the strong bond they had for each other, both as a normal brother and sister might have, and in the special sense made possible by Charles Wallace's "unique" gift.

2. Accept appropriate and well-supported responses.

Page 43

Accept all reasonable and well-supported answers.

Page 44

Perform the conversations in class. Ask students to respond to the conversations in several different ways, such as, "Are the conversations realistic?" or "Are the words the characters say in keeping with their personalities?"